89- 682961

15.96
/1

❖ **Why They Became Fa**

MW00334304

VINCENT VAN GOGH

◆ *Why They Became Famous* ◆

VINCENT VAN GOGH

Sergio Bitossi

English adaption by Vincent Buranelli

Illustrations by Claudio Solarino

Silver Burdett Press

ACKNOWLEDGMENTS
We would like to thank John R. Peters-Campbell, Department of Art,
University of Maryland for his guidance and helpful suggestions.

Library of Congress Cataloging-in-Publication Data

Buranelli, Vincent.
   Vincent van Gogh.

   (Why they became famous)
   Adaptation of: Perchè sono diventati famosi, Van
Gogh / Sergio Bitossi.
   Summary: A biography of the Dutch painter who
was a strange and difficult child, a tortured adult, and
whose genius for expressing his artistic vision was not
appreciated until after his death.
   1. Gogh, Vincent van, 1853-1890 — Juvenile
literature. 2. Painters — Netherlands — Biography —
Juvenile literature. [1. Gogh, Vincent van, 1853-1890.
2. |Artists| I. Bitossi, Sergio. II. Bitossi, Sergio. Perchè
sono diventati famosi, Van Gogh. III. Title. IV. Series.

ND653.G7B77 1987 759.9492 |B| |92| 86-42654
ISBN 0-382-09166-3 (lib. bdg.)
ISBN 0-382-09172-8 (soft)

Impreso por:
Edime Org. Gráfica, S. A.
Móstoles (Madrid)

Encuaderna: Larmor, S. A.
Móstoles (Madrid)

I.S.B.N.: 84-599-1874-2 (cartoné)
I.S.B.N.: 84-599-1875-0 (rústica)
Depósito legal: M. 1333-1987

Impreso en España
Printed in Spain   89- 682961

© Gruppo Editoriale Fabbri S.p.A. 1987

First published in the United States by Silver Burdett Press under license
of Gruppo Editoriale Fabbri S.p.A.

CONTENTS

An Artist's Childhood

The artist clambers over a massive rock formation in one of the wildest regions of France. On his head is a straw hat and with his hands and under his arms he clutches canvas, easel, palette, and tubes of paint. After crossing a brook, he reaches a ravine through which a mountain can be seen in the distance. He stops there, arranges his equipment, and begins to paint the landscape. This painting is known today as *The Ravine*; the artist was Van Gogh.

Vincent van Gogh enjoyed painting under such conditions. As he wrote to a friend, "Such subjects have a melancholy beauty for me. It is great fun to paint in wild spots where it is necessary to prop up the easel with big stones to prevent the wind from knocking it to the ground."

Letters like this one give us an insight into Vincent van Gogh's ideas, and therefore help to explain his paintings. He wrote many letters to his brother Theo, to whom he confided his hopes, fears, ambitions, disappointments, and pleasures. The two brothers were very close, much closer than they were to the other members of their family.

Vincent Willem van Gogh was born on March 30, 1853, in the village of Groot Zundert, in the Dutch province of Brabant, not far from the Belgian border. His father, Theodorus van Gogh, was a preacher in the Dutch Reformed (Calvinist) Church and an easy-going man much respected in the village. Vincent's mother was a woman of strong character who carried on charitable works among the people of the parish. Vincent took after her rather than after his father.

Theodorus van Gogh was not an exceptional preacher, nor did he resemble those of his ancestors who had done very well for themselves in church affairs, business, or sea commerce. Very religious, he took a broad-minded view of theology that enabled him to get along with other denominations. He counted Protestants and Catholics alike among his friends, of whom he had many because of his kindness and friendliness.

He became pastor of Groot Zundert in 1849. Three years later, when he was nearly thirty, he married Anna Cornelia Carbentus, the daughter of a bookbinder from The Hague. Most of those who knew Theodorus and Anna approved of their marriage. "The pastor has chosen a good wife," said one. "After all, they're both faithful members of the Church."

"And they both believe in good works. That will make the pastor's wife as popular as he is in the village."

Those predictions turned out to be true. The parsonage became a place to which any villager could go whenever he or she had a problem. Theodorus and Anna never turned a deaf ear to anyone who needed help. This was a trait they handed on to their son Vincent. When he grew up, he felt as strongly about the suffering of humanity as he did about painting.

Those two themes remained with Vincent through his whole life—the commandment to work for the good of others and the pleasure of expressing his artistic vision by means of his drawing pencil or paint brush. He often united the two themes by depicting on canvas the suffering of the poor—field hands, miners, and tramps.

The slow daily life of Groot Zundert suited young Mrs. van Gogh. With her husband, she took care of the sick, found alms for the poor of the village, and consoled those who suffered bereavement. She looked forward to the birth of her first child—only to endure a dreadful tragedy. On March 30, 1852, she had a son, the first Vincent Willem, but he was dead at birth.

Now the parsonage became a gloomy, mournful place, resounding with constant sobs. For all her character, Anna van Gogh was stricken by the loss of her child. She remained in mourning for quite a long time. The villagers began to fear for her health. Was the pastor's wife losing her mind? When Anna wasn't sitting in the yard under the chestnut tree, staring into space and refusing to talk, she was wandering the fields aimlessly, as if in a trance. The farmers would greet her in their polite, respectful way, but she never answered or even smiled.

"She's crazy!" they began to say in the village.

"Crazy enough to be carted away!"

Only the wiser and more charitable souls among them defended her. "Craziness has nothing to do with it. She's simply a mother blinded by grief, that's all!"

That reason proved to be absolutely right. Later in the year, when Anna felt new life stirring inside her, she seemed to be reborn. She began to laugh and smile again. What's more, all of a sudden she resumed her old way of life. The pastor, not to mention the people of Groot Zundert who had been anxiously concerned about the Van Gogh family during this terrible time, breathed a sigh of relief and rejoiced at the good news.

This time there was no tragedy. Vincent came into the light of day as a big, healthy baby. He wasn't a beautiful baby—not with that flaming red hair, angular face, and freckles all over his body. But Anna beamed just looking at him. As he grew up, on sunny days she would take him around to the village shops or into the countryside to enjoy the open air.

Often, however, Anna led Vincent to the little cemetery to visit his brother's grave. She would place flowers there and talk to Vincent about the lost child after whom he was named.

Those visits had a solemn effect on Vincent. Thoughts of death came to him many times throughout his life. He wondered about the meaning of death and about the fate of one's soul in the next world. That was one reason he always remained so serious in his view of life. He could not shake off the tragedy that had occurred in his own family before he was born. He wondered what it would have been like if he had grown up with an older brother, an experience that fate had denied to him.

More children came to join Vincent in the parsonage—Anna, Theodorus (named after his father but always called Theo), Elizabeth, Wilhelmina, and Cornelius.

As the oldest, Vincent always took the lead when the Van Gogh children played together. They were a lively group, romping around the house, shouting, teasing, fighting, competing for toys and candies, laughing when they got what they wanted, and crying when they didn't.

The poor pastor had trouble finding a quiet corner to write his sermons. Often he had to climb up the rickety, worm-eaten stairs to the attic. At least up there he could escape from his children. But he could not always escape their voices, especially when there was a fight downstairs. The pastor would go over to the tiny window under the eaves and call out gruffly, "Be quiet and behave yourselves."

Almost always he was greeted by a chorus of complaints. Once he heard cries from below and received the following explanation:

"Vincent doesn't want to play with us."

"He stepped on all my flowers and ran away!"

Cornelius, the baby and favorite of the family, pressed up against the fence gate, crying and calling, "Vincent! Wait for me! Take me with you! Vincent!"

All his pleading, however, was in vain because Vincent wanted to be alone. It was one of the times when he preferred to keep to himself, avoiding the company of his brothers and sisters. What appealed to him were the nearby country paths, the brown earth, the smell of the grass, and the chirping from the birds' nests resting on the tree limbs overhead.

"Why do you wander off like that?" his father asked once when the family was at dinner.

The boy usually did not have much to say. How could he explain how he felt? This time he mumbled something about his need to be alone.

"Your brothers and sisters love you," his father insisted. "You should not avoid them."

And Vincent loved them too—he was especially fond of Theo—so it couldn't be that he was angry with his family. No, it was just that their silly games got on his nerves, and the yard around the pastor's house, all fenced-in with only a single chestnut tree, made him feel cooped up. It was like a cage too small for a bird to really flap its wings.

Beyond the gate, on the other hand, lay the splendid countryside, asplash with color and fragrant with the most marvelous smells. The boy roamed over it near and far, his hair tossed by the wind as he fought the strong gusts. He could take his time here, observing and collecting samples for his herb garden or catching insects for his collections, spellbound by the changing color of the sky at sunset.

He watched the red ball descend out of the broad, blue sky and sink into the green of the woods. The colors fascinated him, and the fascination persisted. Later in life he would become a master at placing brilliant hues beside one another in order to make them enhance one another. This is notable in his still life *Sunflower*, with its bold yellows, reds, and greens.

There were times when the curious but reserved boy would slip into the shop of one of the village craftsmen, perhaps a weaver, and stand there silently watching the men at their work. Nothing escaped his sharp eyes, and his concentration was so great that it seemed as if he were holding his breath.

He became a familiar figure, and often the men would speak to him in a friendly way. They realized he was not just a curious child but took a real interest in their work. In short, he was beginning to show that he had the eye of an artist.

Still, he was shy with grown-ups, and he would rarely say anything. He hoped nobody would notice him. When somebody did, he usually walked out of the shop without saying a word. He was afraid he would be laughed at if he said he was interested in arts and crafts.

His parents worried about his desire to keep to himself. "Don't you ever play with the other children of the village?" his father asked.

"I play with caterpillars," Vincent dared to say.

"With caterpillars?" his brothers and sisters sang out in chorus.

"But they're disgusting. I'm afraid of them!" Wilhelmina exclaimed, burying her face in her hands.

Vincent cut them all off by saying, "That's why I don't want you with me!"

The sun was still above the horizon, and Vincent ran off immediately. The path behind the pastor's house led to the moors, covered with heather and full of all sorts of insects. Hurt and confused, the boy raced toward the colors of the horizon. Why *not* bugs? Why didn't anyone else like caterpillars or dragonflies or frogs? It certainly was a shame.

His father, the pastor, commenting from his pulpit on certain verses from the Bible, frequently recalled that all creatures on earth belonged to God and so were worthy of love and respect. Although Theodorus's sermons were far from brilliant, Vincent liked them immensely. He didn't completely understand the meaning and moral of every sermon. But he loved the sounds of the words, sometimes soft and other times mysterious. Vincent heard them all very clearly from a front pew of the church. His father never seemed more admirable than when he spoke to the congregation on Sunday mornings. His father then seemed to be a giant, a man who held the attention of everybody by the power of his preaching.

Then there were joyful moments out in the quiet of the countryside or in his wandering over the moors. Vincent could sit for hours watching the constant coming and going of the ants, the flight of the bees, and the scampering of the field mice. He might have become a naturalist if art had not had a stronger attraction for him.

Vincent's desire for solitude, his habit of wandering on the moors, his passion for the colors he found in nature—these were some of the reasons behind his irregular attendance at the Groot Zundert school. And on days when he didn't play hooky from class, he would often get upset, seemingly over nothing, kicking and punching his classmates.

"He's an unruly child that I don't seem able to handle," the teacher complained to the Reverend Mr. van Gogh. All Theodorus could do was nod silently in agreement, knowing from experience how difficult his son could be. In the end, in order to avoid scandal, he decided to withdraw Vincent from school.

When he heard the news, Vincent, rather than being sorry, was ecstatic. To Theo, who looked at him with disbelief, he said, "That's just how I've always wanted things to end. From the very first day. I'm glad it's over."

The brothers were sitting in the yard under the chestnut tree. "But what," Theo asked in his usual gentle way, "*do* you want from life?"

Theo's question was prompted by his knowledge that Vincent was not just a stupid, lazy dropout. There must be more to it than that.

Of course there was. The budding artist in Vincent knew that painting landscapes can be even more worthwhile than reading school texts and filling notebooks. But he was not yet aware of his true motives.

With Theo's words echoing in his mind, Vincent jumped up suddenly. He was trembling, just like a frightened animal, and he hunched up his shoulders, sputtering, "I—I...," not knowing how to answer his brother, his beloved Theo. At last he gave a shake of his head and said, "I don't know, I don't know. But please, Theo, for heaven's sake, don't ever ask me that again. Never again!"

They were having a very adult conversation, and when he heard his brother make such an anguished plea, Theo felt both sad and afraid.

On the other hand, the family was already used to Vincent's strangeness and his pleading. In fact, they tried as much as possible not to contradict, scold, or punish him. Perhaps they were spoiling him, as the pastor's mother put it one day when she was passing through Groot Zundert and happened to witness one of her grandson's tantrums.

"How can you allow Vincent to turn your house upside down and pick on the rest of the children so?" the grandmother from Breda asked her son and daughter-in-law. "I think you should punish him whenever he quarrels with them."

"He really doesn't mean it," said Anna van Gogh. "Something comes over him. I don't know what it is."

The grandmother turned toward her grandson. "Vincent, do you want to tell me what's bothering you?"

Vincent made no reply, but with all the speed of a furious bull, he charged out the door and out the front gate. In a moment he was gone, hiding out on the moors till nightfall. No one went to look for him; instead they all waited anxiously at the house. Finally he returned, whistling a tune in the moonlight and refusing to give any explanation.

Two Brothers: Vincent and Theo

Despite all his impertinence, temper tantrums, silences, fights, and long absences from home, Vincent grew brighter and more curious—especially about books and drawing. He read many, many books, including some from his father's library, undaunted by even the most difficult theology or morality texts he might happen upon.

And though it was true the boy thought of God more in terms of the things He created in the world and less in terms of the complicated arguments found in philosophy books, God was often in his thoughts. Vincent's idea of God was that which he was brought up to believe: God was good, powerful, and inflexible, demanding much of His creatures but also rewarding those who did not falter in their pursuit of goodness.

He confided this to Theo, with whom he was so very close. More and more of late, he had begun to take his younger brother with him on his long walks. They talked much about religion.

"I agree with Father," Vincent said. "Our church tells us to read the Bible and follow its teachings. That's what I believe. My favorite text is the Sermon on the Mount. I intend to obey it to the best of my ability."

Theo listened with admiration. Except for their wavy reddish hair, the two brothers didn't look at all alike. Sensitive as well as orderly, like the Pastor, Theo listened, excited by Vincent's words, yet hesitant about so complete a commitment to the words of the Bible.

"Father says God is everywhere," Theo pointed out.

"I believe it, Theo, because I feel I'm in touch with Him everywhere. I see Him in the fields of grass, in the colors of the flowers, in the sunlight. That flutter of wind rustling the leaves—that's God talking to me."

And then on a piece of paper Vincent would quickly sketch a bird in flight, the leaves of a tree rippling in the wind, or a flower opening to the sunlight.

"That's good!" Theo exclaimed each time. "That's really good!"

Their mother as well was amazed by these drawings and tried quietly to give Vincent a quick hug, knowing that he hated "mushiness" of any sort. His reaction was very different, however, when she asked to keep some of his sketches for her dresser drawer. Then he was very pleased and handed them over with a soft, disarming look.

Mother and son very often communicated by looks and glances. There were certain long, silent moments, at lunch or dinner, when love, pity, and mutual understanding were present in equal measure. Anna van Gogh did not have it in her to scold Vincent, even at those times when a scolding was clearly needed. Theodorus van Gogh got exasperated and accused his wife of being too soft on the boy, saying, "Vincent needs a good example, as well as discipline and strictness at his age. He's not a child anymore. He's almost a man. We both should realize it. We should let him know when we disapprove of what he's done."

Mrs. van Gogh sighed but rarely said anything critical of her son's behavior. Her common reply to those who complained about him was, "Well, that's precisely why he needs so much love and attention!"

"I see," commented her husband, which meant that he saw she was not on his side. Yet when he was certain that his son loved to draw, Theodorus van Gogh breathed a sigh of relief and encouraged Vincent to keep at it.

It's very possible that in his heart of hearts he really didn't care for Vincent's sketches—the harsh outlines of figures, the lack of subtle shading, the mutations that tree trunks, bushes, and animal faces suffered at the hands of the young artist. It was almost as if every living thing were full of anger and restlessness, trampled by Vincent's will and then whimsically recreated. Nonetheless, the father applauded all his son's efforts, and upon seeing each new drawing, he would say encouragingly, "Well done! Keep it up. Who knows—maybe you'll be a famous painter some day."

Vincent must have been pleased by these words, but as far as we know, he never said so. He was too withdrawn, too bound up in his own thoughts to make any reply even to his father. Also, he was still young, and the future seemed far away. If, for example, Theo said to him, "One day you'll leave Groot Zundert and I'll have to search the world over to find you," Vincent would shake his head and deny it. He had, in fact, no great desire to go away from Brabant at this time. The Dutch province was often windy, rainy, and cold, but this climate fitted in with his temperament. He found Brabant enchanting under its mantle of snow and mysterious under its blanket of fog. Yes, Vincent loved his native land and even the dark shadows cast by the roofs of the houses.

It was also true, however, that when his eyes began to scan the horizon, or when the north wind began to howl, he was irresistibly drawn to the paths that led toward the red glow of the sunset, or into the gusts of the cold wind. He was looking for something, and he could not be certain that he would find it in Brabant. Years later he found what he wanted among the artists in France. There he discovered the delights of a warm sun and balmy breezes.

How the change came about can be followed in Vincent's famous *Letters to Theo*, a collection that at least in terms of sincerity and poetry is equal to his paintings. Some themes are constant throughout his life. Both as a child and as a mature artist, he would search for truth, freedom, and new ways to express himself. He would, at the same time, experience many places and much unhappiness along the way.

But let's not get ahead of the story. Now it is only October 1, 1864, and Vincent is leaving Groot Zundert to attend (as a live-in student) an art school directed by the painter Jean Provily, in the nearby city of Zevenbergen. This is his farewell to childhood.

Vincent would remain at Mr. Provily's school for four years. He grew up, becoming more mature, making himself amenable to the other students, showing respect to the teachers. He read widely and applied himself to his studies. He learned English, French, and German. Continuing with his drawing, he did studies from models or from nature as required in class.

He went back to Groot Zundert during summer vacations. Once home, he became the old difficult Vincent van Gogh again and was soon back to his old habit of taking long, aimless walks. Restless and once more withdrawn, he would nonetheless pour out his soul to Theo, his one and lifelong friend.

"I missed you, Theo. And at Zevenbergen I also missed these trees bending in the wind and the wild heather on the moors. In summer, the countryside around Zevenbergen is lush with green and flowers everywhere, but I don't care. It's not a place where I want to live."

In Groot Zundert, some of Vincent's worst habits came back. As of old, he tended to be quarrelsome with his relatives and with the villagers. These were no longer childish tantrums, however. He was still looking for something that eluded him, but now it became obvious that he suffered from psychological problems that caused him to erupt into a frenzy when he felt thwarted.

Theodorus van Gogh was harder on his son and less willing to let things go on as they were. One day he said to him, "Work is an unavoidable part of man's existence. You're sixteen now, Vincent, and it's high time you began to experience this on your own. You must go into adult work that will teach you the meaning of responsibility."

Taken by surprise, Vincent waited to hear more. He had no desire to return to Zevenbergen, but he wanted to know what alternative his father had in mind for him. The Pastor continued: "Your Uncle Cent [short for Vincent] has sold his art gallery to Goupil's of Paris. In The Hague, Goupil's has a major branch office, and Uncle Cent has arranged for you to join the staff. I think you might do well in the business. After all, you like art, and now you'll be surrounded by it all the time. What do you say? How do you feel about it?"

Vincent said he was intrigued by the idea that he, an artist, should become an art dealer.

"Good. And since I was sure you'd agree completely, a couple of days ago I wrote to Uncle Cent, who has seen to everything. You've just been hired by the Goupil gallery, and you are to leave for The Hague tomorrow."

"Tomorrow early?" Vincent inquired. "Does Theo know?" He was concerned that he might have to leave without seeing Theo.

"What does Theo have to do with anything? You, my boy, are our eldest, and therefore it's up to you to prepare the way for your brothers and sisters. Make them proud of you by working hard and not being foolish. But yes, Theo does know, and he'll be on hand when you leave tomorrow."

And so Vincent went to work at Goupil's in The Hague. He lived up to his father's expectations and to the promises made to Theo, who wrote to him regularly. For the first time in his life, Vincent felt at peace with himself. Nothing happened to upset him, and so he got along well with his superiors, his fellow salesmen, and the clients who came to Goupil's to buy works of art.

The real point was that Vincent now lived among sculptures and paintings by the world's most renowned artists. He worked diligently, happy to be doing something that pleased him. His eyes took in all of it. He was curious and enchanted. Oils, lithographs, female nudes, twilight pastoral scenes, even the gigantic canvases depicting important battles—all attracted his attention and interest. He would write to Theo—who would find it hard to believe him: "My life is going smoothly and is very quiet. I find my job fulfilling, even if it's hard. Sometimes it's difficult not to

feel envious, working around all those paintings by famous painters. But I couldn't ask for more, Theo. I'm happy!"

Meanwhile, due to money problems, the Van Gogh family had left the parsonage in Groot Zundert and moved to Helvoirt, another village in the province of Brabant, not far from the town of Tilburg. In 1872, Vincent returned home for a brief vacation and immediately took off for Oisterwijk, where Theo was taking some educational courses. It was a wonderful and emotional reunion for the two brothers, who gave each other a big long bear hug.

"Theo," Vincent said in his usual rash manner, "you just have to come with me. Back to The Hague. Right now. I need you."

But their father—burdened with children and debts—also needed Theo, who one year later was hired, just as Vincent had been, by Goupil's. This would have been all right, except that Theo went to the branch in Brussels, and Vincent was still in The Hague. Moreover, Vincent was about to leave for London. His apprenticeship as an art dealer had ended, and as a sign of recognition for his hard work, Goupil's was promoting him to a prestigious position in its London gallery.

Vincent arrived in London in May of 1873, when he was twenty years old. For the first few months of his stay, things went smoothly and he was happy. He wrote to his brother, "My dear Theo, this is really an easy place to work. I never begin before nine in the morning, and I have all of Saturday afternoon to myself. What's more, London represents new and exciting horizons."

He wasn't wasting any time. He visited all the famous museums and rarely missed any of the important antique shows. He had a rather mixed reaction to English painting at first, but he later fell in love with Constable, Reynolds, Gainsborough, and Turner. He could stand for hours in the rain, looking in the windows of *Graphic* or the *London News* displaying the drawings of artists from the Continent.

That spring, he started a small collection of engravings, and his letters to Theo reveal how proud he was of it. As September drew near, he moved out of the small hotel that was costing him too much and into rooms rented in the home of a Mrs. Loyer, a widow whose husband had been a minister. Mrs. Loyer had a beautiful young daughter named Ursula. Vincent immediately renamed her "the angel of babies," as she worked in a nursery school. Swept off his feet by the girl, Vincent watched her move about the parlor as if under a spell. Shy and awkward, he found it difficult to tell her how he felt. After many months, he managed to say that he wanted to marry her. To his dismay, Ursula laughed at him.

"Oh Vincent!" Ursula said, touched and yet finding it all so funny. "Dear, sweet Vincent, I've been engaged for some time now and am about to be married!"

The unexpected blow that struck him—these words, her tone of voice, and the peals of laughter—was a cruel one indeed. Not only were his feelings hurt, but he felt like a fool for not realizing that she was already engaged to be married. He felt stunned as the fact came home to him that the hopes he had held for a new, happier life were based on an illusion. Fury welled up inside of him, and he started to speak angry words.

Ursula refused to listen. Frightened by his reaction, she rushed out of the room, leaving Vincent with the realization that Ursula was not for him.

With a deeply wounded heart, and badly damaged pride, Vincent returned home at the end of June, 1874, for a brief vacation. His parents were astonished to see that he had returned to being the Vincent of times past: sullen, impossible, and quick-tempered. They couldn't believe it, and they badgered him with questions. Vincent, however, could not bring himself to tell them about Ursula Loyer. He shrugged his shoulders and with hardly a word went off down the country paths in the direction of the woods or the moors, just as he had done as a boy.

When Theo, to whom Vincent had confided the truth, wrote and told their father about Vincent's disaster at love, the Reverend van Gogh tried to console him. Furthermore, when the director of the Goupil gallery in London wrote asking Vincent to return, his father—fearing for him and his health—asked Vincent's sister Anna to accompany him back to England.

To avoid running into Ursula, the two found rooms in Kensington New Road, far from Mrs. Loyer's. Vincent returned to work, although it was immediately plain to everyone that he had lost his will and desire to succeed in the business. He was cranky, always on edge, and likely to avoid customers or give one-word answers.

Even with the director and his co-workers, Vincent was rude and abrupt, refusing to listen to anyone, although all they wanted was to give him some well-meant advice. More than once they found him tucked in a dark corner reading some just-published novel and off in another world, despite the customers who were anxious to buy pictures and asking for help.

"Mr. van Gogh!" an attendant would call brusquely.

"Eh?" he would respond shortly. And he would show no enthusiasm as he went to wait on a customer.

If it had not been for the influence and reputation of his Uncle Cent, Vincent would have been fired on the spot. His uncle was well aware of the reasons behind Vincent's poor attitude, and he worked to obtain his transfer to the main Goupil gallery in Rue Chaptal, Paris.

"The Paris museums and the chance to meet new, exciting artists will help you to forget what's past," Uncle Cent said to comfort his nephew. Then with a sigh he added, "Or anyway, I hope so, for your sake, my dear Vincent, and for your family's peace of mind. This is a fresh opportunity for you. Please do the best you can to make it a success."

Life Among the Lowly

In 1875, Vincent moved to Paris and rented a small room in the part of the city known as Montmartre. In his spare time he visited the Louvre Museum and attended other painting exhibitions held in the city. But, in any case, he stayed well out of the debates on art and cultural events of the day that were taking the city by storm. On the contrary, Vincent—unlike the other painters and the writers—was desperately looking for solitude and a sense of being spiritually at peace.

More than anything else he wanted to find God. Together with Harry Gladwell, who worked with him at Goupil's, Vincent would read and discuss Bible verses by the hour, or go to pray at the nearby Anglican church, joining in zealously when it came time to sing the Sunday hymns.

Although this religious fervor helped Vincent to get over Ursula, it also led him to want more time for himself, greater freedom, and broader horizons than his job allowed. Impulsively—as was his custom—Vincent resigned from Goupil's on April 1, 1876, and left for England.

In Ramsgate, a small town in Kent near the Straits of Dover, Vincent found work as an assistant instructor in the Reverend Mr. Stokes's school, where he taught

languages. Later he was hired at another school as an assistant to the Reverend Mr. Jones, a Methodist preacher who lived in the extremely poor quarter of London called Isleworth. Although life there was very hard, Vincent never complained, having decided that God had elected him as His disciple and that he would obey the Lord's wishes by dedicating his life to preaching and to helping the needy.

Theodorus van Gogh was concerned about his son's sudden decision. His concern for Vincent's health and religious fervor made him decide to help out by once again asking a favor of Uncle Cent. And so it was that in July, 1878, Vincent went to Brussels and entered the Flemish Evangelical School for three months of lessons to earn a license as a lay preacher.

Here again his passion and temperament got him into trouble, with the result that at the end of the course the instructors deemed him unfit to be a preacher and refused to grant him the degree. Crushed by yet another disappointment, Vincent wandered like a hobo around southern Belgium until he reached the mining region of the Borinage, near the French border.

"Here at last!" Vincent thought, feeling inspired. "This is where God was trying to lead me. And this is where I plan to stay and preach to the miners, my brothers. I'll try to help them in this wasteland of dead grass and coal dust. Everybody else seems to have forgotten them. But I won't! Oh Lord, that is my pledge—to do Your work!"

For the time being he settled in Paturages, staying with a vendor named Van der Haegen; but then, in January, 1879, the Evangelical School Committee of Brussels offered him a six-month position as a lay preacher in Wasmes in the mining region of Mons.

To humble himself to the task and also to share fully in the miserable conditions the miners had to live in, Vincent gave up his rented room in the home of a baker named Denis and took shelter in a broken-down shack, sleeping on a pile of straw. Overwhelmed by the poverty and suffering all around him, Vincent plunged into a campaign of compassion and good works—preaching, helping the sick and the injured, giving away what little money he had to those who needed it more than he did.

At the same time, he began to make pencil sketches of the hard, desperate faces he saw as well as of the desolate, scarred landscape. His drawing *The Miner*, revealing their dismal lives, dates from this period.

He had never, of course, lost interest in painting. In Paris, for instance, besides the thousand masterpieces displayed in the Louvre, he had seen an exhibition of paintings by Camille Corot that had impressed him greatly. And during his stay in England, he had visited Hampton Court many times to study the masters of the Italian Renaissance and to examine the works of Dutch painters, such as Holbein and Rembrandt.

It was also true that he had never stopped drawing. His technique got better, and he found new ways to express in art the ideas in his mind.

His religious work, however, didn't allow him much time for study or art. During the months he spent in Wasmes, Vincent became thin and worn-out. He ate very little and badly. With his tattered clothes and unkempt beard, it was almost as if he himself were a miner. All the while, his eyes were burning with passion. He was reaching the point of mystical fanaticism. The authorities of the theological school in Brussels were not pleased, and at the end of the six months, they decided that Vincent must go, to be replaced by somebody more respectable.

This was another terrible shock, and again he reacted violently. "It's not possible! It's not fair!" he cried out in anger and desperation. But that was that, and Vincent simply had to adjust to the fact. Adjustment was extremely difficult for him. "Please, God Almighty," he prayed during one long, sleepless night, "remove all bitterness from my heart and let me hear Your voice to guide me."

After talking to a preacher, the Reverend Pieterson, who had more faith in him than did his superiors, and swallowing his pride, Vincent decided to stay on as a preacher in the Borinage region, even if without pay or official title. From Wasmes he moved to Cuesmes, a nearby village, and lived first with a minister named Frank and then with the miner Charles Decrucq. He was alone in the midst of misery; even his beloved Theo, who strongly disapproved of his decision to stay, had stopped writing. Vincent's world seemed to have caved in on top of him. He was often hungry, and feverish.

He might have given way to complete despair if it had not been for his art. He was beginning to mature into an artist for whom the greatest relief was the painting he did in his spare time.

In pursuit of his art, Vincent walked all the way to Carrieres near the English Channel to see the painter Jules Breton, whom he admired greatly. Vincent took

some of his own works, hoping for encouragement from Breton. But when he reached the front door of Breton's luxurious home, he suddenly felt weak, and his hands began to tremble as if he were delirious. He did not have the courage to reach out and ring the doorbell. He turned and fled down the street in a panic. His fear seems ironic today, because he became a much greater artist than Breton.

For several days afterward, Vincent wandered around the countryside near Cuesmes, sleeping in the fields. He had become by this time little more than a miserable tramp.

Finally, in July, 1880, an affectionate letter and some money arrived from Theo, and things no longer appeared so grim. With new zeal, Vincent began to draw again, sometimes portraits of the miners as before and sometimes copies of works by Breton and Millet. Eventually, he left the mining region for Brussels and enrolled in the Academy of Fine Arts. This time he made an effort to establish contact with the art world, becoming friends with Ridder Anton van Rappard, a Dutch painter about his age.

In Etten, the new home of the Reverend Mr. van Gogh and his family, Vincent spent a brief but happy time vacationing with Rappard in the spring of 1881. They would go out together into the countryside to paint, to talk about light and color, and to discuss the other artists they admired.

"Millet! Millet is wonderful!" Vincent said.

"And Daumier! And Dupré!" Rappard added.

"All three of them!" Vincent concluded.

At the start of the summer, Vincent's cousin Kee—the daughter of another minister named Stricker—came for a visit. When Vincent saw her, recently widowed and with a small son, he fell head over heels in love. In an outburst of violent emotion, he soon told her of his feelings. Startled and rather upset by this new turn of events, Kee not only firmly refused Vincent but quickly packed her bags and returned to Amsterdam.

Very hurt but refusing to take "no" for an answer, Vincent followed her there and insisted on seeing and talking to her. In the presence of the Reverend Mr. Stricker and his wife, Kee refused once again, at which point Vincent stuck his hand into the hot flame of the oil lamp and shouted at her and her terrified relatives. "Let the fire burn me, I don't care! This is proof of my love for you, Kee. This is proof of my pain. What else must I do to show you, Kee?"

The news of Vincent's gesture made many people believe that he was losing his mind. But in spite of it all, he was still painting.

Van Gogh moved to The Hague in January, 1882. There he took lessons in painting from Anton Mauve, a cousin by marriage. A well-known Dutch painter of the time, the man tried his best to help Vincent develop his painting technique. Unfortunately, Mauve's suggestions and criticisms were met with Vincent's characteristic anger and the relationship ended. In spite of this and similar incidents when others offered him instruction, Vincent remained dedicated to his art.

In 1883 Van Gogh moved from The Hague to the remote and lonely town of Drenthe in the northwestern part of Holland. The time he spent there did not prove to be productive in a creative sense, and Vincent left after just three months.

By this time the Van Gogh family had moved to Neunen, a small town with a sizable Catholic community. Upon leaving Drenthe, Vincent joined his family in their

new home, and stayed for two years. While living in Neunen he produced over a hundred paintings, watercolors, and drawings. The villagers became accustomed to seeing him at his easel in the open air. Some found it difficult to believe that so quick-tempered a man could discipline himself to the task of patiently filling in a blank canvas with figures or of applying just the right colors to still lifes such as baskets of fruit.

But, of course, this was not work for Vincent. He reveled in his art, and no hours were more pleasant to him than those he spent with a paint brush in his hand and a half-completed picture on his easel.

The minister's house that had been assigned to the Reverend Mr. van Gogh was one of the nicest in Neunen. Located on the main street, it had two stories, each with five large windows, plus an ivy-covered facade and lush, shady yard. Vincent was allowed to turn the laundry room into a studio. Finally king of his own little world, Vincent moved in with his piles of canvases and boxes, his easels and paints, as well as the oil paintings and watercolors he had completed thus far. Chaos appeared to reign, and everything was bathed in the smell of turpentine. But there was method in his disorder, for he knew exactly what he was doing when he began work on a picture.

Almost every day, even when it looked like rain, Vincent would walk out into the surrounding countryside in order to sketch the farmers, with their lined faces, or the weavers at work, or the miners returning home from their shifts with blackened faces. The artist's hand in these drawings was, as before, expert but tormented. He favored dark, muddy, earthy tones, although his brother Theo had written to him from Paris about the radiant light in paintings by the Impressionists. "That's how my spirit is," Vincent would confess to Theo. "I'm restless, afflicted, unable to rise into the glowing optimism that you seem to enjoy."

On January 17, 1884, his mother fell and fractured her leg. During the long convalescence when she was confined to her bed, Vincent took loving care of her, attending to her every need. For her amusement, he made pen-and-ink drawings of the little Neunen church, with trees and people in the background. She enjoyed the drawings, and her enjoyment helped to make her well.

This happy time for the Van Gogh family proved to be short-lived. By May, and after many arguments and angry rows with his father, Vincent had moved his studio over the home of the Catholic sexton, Herr Schafrath.

"At least here I'm not forced to listen to the complaints of those who have no conception of the problems that hound me," Vincent confessed to his friend Rappard, who came to see him not long after his move.

"They accuse me of sponging off Theo and not knowing how to sell a single painting. Someone is always keeping an eye on me as they would with someone who'd just gotten out of the insane asylum. And then they all feel they have to tell me what clothes I should wear, or what hat, or kind of cane to carry!"

All this was true. The solidly middle-class Van Gogh family had a hard time trying to understand Vincent's large, restless spirit and the ideas he was putting into his art. Even though they were willing to give him a home and help him out with money when he needed it, they nevertheless remained highly critical of the way he lived and the comments he made. Theodorus van Gogh in particular remained puzzled and annoyed by his eldest son.

In August, 1884, a woman of Nuenen named Margot Begemann tried to commit suicide. Almost immediately word spread that Vincent van Gogh was responsible, for it was known that he was romantically interested in her. It was thought that his persistent attentions had been too much for Margot, who was eight years older than Vincent.

Actually, the fault lay with the two families, for both opposed the marriage of the couple. Mr. Begemann had gone so far as to forbid his daughter to have anything to do with "that damned crazy painter." The Reverend Mr. van Gogh, on the other hand, had warned Vincent against marrying a woman so much older than himself, adding that Margot was from a poor family, so she would not bring him any substantial dowry to help with his financial problem.

The continual arguments with his father and with the rest of the family depressed Vincent. For a while he was even unable to paint. Fortunately, there were letters from Theo, which always arrived with money, sound advice, useful information, and affectionate encouragement. From Paris, where he was doing well, working at the same Goupil gallery that had previously employed his brother, Theo wrote, "I have faith in you and in your talent, Vincent. It's not just because you're my brother that I can say that! My instinct as an art dealer also tells me that one day you're going to find it in you to express on canvas all your love and all your endless suffering. That day will be one of the most wonderful ever."

Theo's letters had the effect of a magic potion. They enabled Vincent to shake off his depression, forget the bitterness he felt toward his peevish family, and attack his work with all the energy he had displayed in the past.

The fall of 1884 was a very creative time for Vincent. From landscapes and scenes showing weavers and farmers at work, he moved to life studies of figures and heads. "I want to paint at least 50 of them during the long winter in Nuenen," he said excitedly to Rappard, as well as in a letter to Theo.

Then suddenly on March 26, 1885, the Reverend Mr. van Gogh suffered a stroke—without ever having manifested any sign of the illness before—and died. Even though Vincent had clashed violently with his father at times, he felt intense pain and sorrow at his passing and could hardly find the strength to follow the funeral procession to the cemetery. As the casket was being lowered into the grave, Vincent whispered, "May the Lord grant you peace, my dear father. And may the first Vincent who has been waiting for you there in Heaven help you to forgive and love the Vincent who is still here, suffering in this vale of tears."

After consoling the rest of the family, Vincent disappeared from sight, holing up in his studio and not emerging for a number of days. He was haunted by memories of Theodorus van Gogh, not only his father but also the preacher from whom he had learned to revere the Bible and follow its teachings.

The First Masterpiece: The Potato Eaters

Vincent had made some friends in the Nuenen area. The group was made up of young men who met each other buying paints and other art supplies in the store owned by Jean Baaiens: Hermans was a goldsmith, Willem van der Wakker worked in the post office, Dimmen Gestel helped his father, a printer, and Anton Kerssemakers was a wholesaler who dealt in tobacco. They had asked Vincent to teach them the rudiments of painting for not too high a price, and he had willingly accepted.

None of the others had anything like his talent. They were therefore glad to have him show them his techniques for mixing paints on their palettes, sketching in the outline of a picture, and then filling it in with the proper combination of colors.

When asked why he used dark, solemn colors, he commented, "They express my feelings just now, but the day may come when I will switch to lighter colors. Always, an artist should express his feelings of the moment as honestly as he can."

Each day Vincent was getting more and more involved in his painting and in certain fundamental problems posed by art in general. From his reading of essays by the painter Eugène Delacroix and the art historian Eugène Fromentin, for example, he was convinced that between color and music there existed a sort of corresponding relationship that was closer than was commonly believed. It was for this reason that he decided to study piano and sight-reading with a music teacher named Van Sanden, although soon even Vincent was forced to admit that the results of this "experiment" were rather disappointing.

"No, not like that! Not like that!" the maestro would shout at his fiery, maddening pupil. "You can't pound on the keys like that. You, dear sir, are not yet Richard Wagner. And perhaps you will never be."

The lessons came to an abrupt end, and Vincent never did master music. During April and May, 1885, he painted *The Potato Eaters*, the famous work dating from his Dutch period. The paint was hardly dry when he took it to show Kerssemakers in Eindhoven. He sent off a lithograph of the work to Rappard, but contrary to all expectation, his friend proved to be highly critical and even sarcastic.

This masterpiece shows a poor family at dinner, having nothing to eat but a dish of potatoes. The suffering of poverty and a hard life are starkly revealed in their faces, which Vincent portrayed in the somber colors he preferred at this stage in his career. The subject and the treatment were too much for Rappard to accept.

After five years of close friendship, Vincent broke with Rappard over *The Potato Eaters*. "He doesn't understand my kind of realism," Vincent would say to his friends. Which was true.

In the fall of 1885, Vincent moved to Antwerp. Partly this was because of gossip about him in Nuenen. He got tired of hearing that he must be immoral because of his vagabond life, and he resented it when a curate forbade parishioners to pose for him.

But also, Vincent's art career was moving into another phase. He wanted to study more of the old masters, which he could do in the museums and art galleries of Antwerp. He wanted to learn more and, from this knowledge, to develop new techniques. And so he moved to the Belgian city and started a new life.

Arriving in Antwerp one rainy day in November, Vincent van Gogh rented a small room in Longue Rue des Images, in the house of Madame and Monsieur Brandel. He almost seemed to be a new man, thanks to his new surroundings. Confident that he would be able to sell a few paintings, Vincent made a real effort to be nice to people, go to art galleries, and be seen in the company of influential critics and popular painters.

Many times, and with growing interest, he visited the museums in Antwerp and began to study closely the works of Peter Paul Rubens. He was especially struck by the active gestures of the figures, the emotional expressions, and the sumptuous colors. Of Rubens he would say, "He is the painter who tried more than any other to express, and realistically represent, an atmosphere of utter joy, tranquility, and pain, through the use of incredible combinations of color."

Vincent often stood spellbound and moved, in front of the painting *The Deposition of Christ* by Rubens. There was no getting around the power of this picture. Guided by what he learned from the great Flemish master, Vincent wiped the dark, somber colors off his palette and began instead to highlight his paintings with bright, vivid hues.

Rubens was not the only inspiration to help him decide on such a radical change. Wandering down by the port, Vincent came across cheap Chinese and Japanese prints and was struck by how gay, bright, and whimsical they were. "They're pure poetry," he thought with admiration. "Created out of nothing, but they immediately capture your heart."

On January 18, 1886, Vincent enrolled in the first-level class at the School of Fine Arts. His teacher was Charles M. M. Verlat, a mediocre painter, all things considered— as conventional as he was uninspired. Naturally, Vincent rebelled against his teacher's conformist and academic approach—only to be failed on the extrance exams for the second-level course.

There wasn't a drop of energy left in him to be spent railing against Verlat or the other reactionaries at the School of Fine Arts. Underfed, worn-out from the heavy course-load, and coughing because of too much smoking, Vincent became ill. He had to stay in bed. Dr. Cavenaille, who treated him, had a reputation for loving art more than cash payments. Vincent was quick to forewarn him. "Look here, Doctor, I can't possibly pay for these visits."

"But I'm sure that you'll be very capable of painting my portrait for me once you're well," Dr. Cavenaille replied. And as promised, the portrait was completed. Since then, however, every effort to track it down has been unsuccessful. Perhaps it was destroyed. Or perhaps it's still lying forgotten in someone's attic.

Many other pictures by Van Gogh were lost during his lifetime. When in May, 1886, his mother had to leave the minister's house in Nuenen, she left hundreds of Vincent's drawings, watercolors, and oils in the care of a village shopkeeper. This gold mine later fell into the hands of a junk dealer. He burned a number of the works and sold off the rest to a tailor from Breda for the ridiculous price of ten centimes each!

Vincent responded well to Dr. Cavenaille's treatment and by the end of February was back on his feet. As soon as he was standing and walking again, he decided that he would not spend any more time cooped up in a closed room in order to get well. Besides, he was set on leaving Antwerp immediately with the idea of going to Paris to study with Fernand Cormon, a traditionalist painter highly rated by the critics and popular with the buyers.

Vincent wanted to analyze Cormon's works and learn the secret of his success. He left that very night for Paris without telling anyone. Only after he arrived did he write Theo a note, arranging to meet him at a certain time in the Carré Room at the Louvre. Theo was utterly amazed, but he had learned to expect anything from his older brother. The two held a joyous reunion. Theo told of his success as an art dealer in Paris, and Vincent confided his hopes for a renewal of his career in the French capital.

"Oh, Theo!" Vincent's morale was sky-high as he said this. "When I'm with you, I feel like a new man. I know you'll be a good influence on me and keep me in line. Besides, I expect you'll refine my tastes and improve my standards a bit."

Theo managed a small gallery on Boulevard Montmartre for Goupil's, and there, or in the nearby restaurants and bars, he would often run into daring young Impressionists and their friends. "A very nice bunch of people," he told Vincent. "And all highly talented. Maybe they're a little too hotheaded and controversial—although they've got good reason to be, of course. They're bringing new life to painting, and it's taking Paris a long time to wake up to the fact. I'd go so far as to say that the critics and gallery owners are competing to see who can snub or belittle them the most."

During all of 1886, hardly a night went by when Vincent did not encounter one of the Impressionists or their literary friends. He knew Monet, Pissarro, Renoir, and Degas, as well as Toulouse-Lautrec, Seurat, Sisley, and Signac. These are now great names in the history of art, but at that time most of them were struggling to make a success of painting.

Vincent, the unknown from the Low Countries, was shy in their company. He said little. He preferred to listen, and what he heard made a lasting impression on him. His new friends—with their radical theories, and brighter, more luminous colors than anything he had seen in the Dutch tradition—fascinated him, and they taught him much about the direction in which the art of the nineteenth century was moving.

In Paris, Vincent did a number of self-portraits. They portray a man with rough-hewn features. He has a jutting jaw, beetling eyebrows, bony cheeks, and a receding hairline that accentuates the backward thrust of the skull. His mouth is pursed as if he were contemplating some profound moral or artistic problem. His eyes are deep-set, and they are fixed in a stare that tells of much suffering and much thought about the meaning of suffering.

But Vincent brought a lighter touch to lighter subjects. He did a number of pictures for the walls of the café Le Tambourin, a cabaret he frequented; *Interior of a Restaurant* is an example. One of his most familiar paintings of a lighter subject dates from a year or two later; this, *Fishing Boats on the Beach at Saintes-Maries*, he painted in the south of France.

In the winter of 1886–87, Vincent met Paul Gauguin, another artist who was trying to find his direction in art. They became good friends and talked endlessly about their paintings and their hopes. They both were making their way beyond Impressionism into Postimpressionism. Because of this friendship, Vincent was able to exhibit several paintings in a shop owned by Gauguin's father. (There were no buyers.)

Vincent also met Émile Bernard, another painter with whom he became friendly. They used to go out to paint together in a Paris suburb along the Seine River where Bernard's parents lived. Vincent enjoyed these outings, from which he came back refreshed and ready to attack more blank canvases in his Paris studio.

His evenings in the city were usually spent at the café Le Tambourin, which was on the Boulevard Clichy and run by an Italian woman, once a model for Degas, named Agostina Segatori. He met many of his friends at this café, but the main reason for going there was his romantic interest in Agostina. She felt the same way about him, and they got along together very well.

In fact, she commissioned Vincent to do the artwork for her café. He decorated the walls with scenes of Paris. At the same time, he introduced her to Japanese prints, which he bought at Bing's, a curio shop in the Rue de Provence. These prints hung beside his oil paintings in the café Le Tambourin.

Agostina was thrilled by the pictures Vincent painted for her. She pointed them out to her other patrons, many of whom were also impressed. At last she and Vincent decided to hold an exhibition of his works at the café, along with some contributions by his friends.

"If I show some paintings," he said to her, "I'm sure Bernard will, too. We could also invite Gauguin and Toulouse-Lautrec, and maybe one or two of the Impressionists. We'll call ourselves 'The Painters from the City Streets.' It should be interesting."

As it turned out, Toulouse-Lautrec was the only big name who offered works to the exhibition at Le Tambourin. The others were Vincent, Bernard, and a painter named Anquetin. The exhibition brought them many compliments but few francs. One of Vincent's contributions was A *Woman in the Café Le Tambourin*.

Vincent in Arles: Sunlight and Sea

This magical time didn't last for long, however. On February 20, 1888, following yet another terrible fit of depression, Van Gogh abruptly left Paris and Agostina, and fled southward toward the Mediterranean Sea, settling in the town of Arles, which Toulouse-Lautrec had told him about. From the Hotel-Restaurant Carrel at 30 Rue Cavalerie, he wrote to his brother, insisting he had made the right decision. He said in one letter, "I need sunlight and warmth. I want my paintings to be bright with sun, sea, and sky. Provence does indeed have something Japanese about it."

The climate of Provence and the early blossoming of the fruit trees inspired Vincent to work nonstop on an unbelievable number of paintings. He would get up early in the morning and go out to wander through the countryside or stand enchanted by the view of the boats working along the banks of the Rhone River. In the evening he would drag himself back to the hotel utterly exhausted, but if he still had enough strength left, he would attach two small candles to his hat rim and continue to paint anyway.

Friends in Paris sent word that at the *Salon* of independent artists he had three works on display—two street scenes of the city and a still life. "A good omen!" he thought.

At the beginning of May, he rented the entire right wing of Ginoux's house on Place Lamartine. For Vincent it instantly became the "Yellow House" because of its yellow exterior. In his four-room home, Vincent hoped to start a small commune made up of painter friends, for he was getting rather lonely. He wrote, for example, to Gauguin, "You'll be the first, if you'd like to come. You'll love the light and beauty of the Midi [the South], and you'll want to stay forever in my Yellow House."

This building is immortalized in his painting *The Small House of Vincent at Arles*. He decorated it with paintings of sunflowers that show as well as any of his canvases how he had abandoned the somber colors of the past for the brilliant hues he saw all around him in Arles.

Occasionally the Ginoux family would ask him to dinner, as they were now his friends. Amused and fascinated, Madame Ginoux consented to sit for Vincent's painting *The Woman of Arles*. Vincent also met a second lieutenant in the French Zouaves (a kind of foreign legion). The officer, whose name was Milliet, could not completely appreciate Vincent's art, yet wanted Vincent to teach him to draw. Milliet did not have much talent, and the lessons did not go on for very long.

One day Vincent would be out in the orchard, between the fruit trees, and the next day in the tall meadow grass or beyond, in the fields of wheat. By mid-June, he had wandered as far as the fishing village of Saintes-Maries-de-la-Mer, irresistibly drawn to the boats and to the smell of the sea that always seemed to relax him. However, his favorite spot was not the sea but at Montmajour, a hamlet close to Arles, where he painted dozens of bright, vibrant landscapes.

Being in the South of France was doing Vincent a world of good. He felt better than he had in his entire life, and he was moved by a driving compulsion to paint the beauty of Provence. Every day was a new adventure. He wrote to Theo of the thrill of seeing "fields green and yellow as far as the eye reaches."

Theo's letters came regularly, and they indirectly gave Vincent another subject to paint. He was struck by the appearance of the mailman who delivered the letters, and persuaded him to pose for a portrait. After that, Vincent did the mailman's wife and children. "I've captured the entire Roulin family," as he put it. In fact, he painted the mailman half a dozen times.

Drawings of the outdoors proliferated—*Orchard*, *Cornfield*, *Fruit Trees*, *Fading Daylight*, and many others with similar titles. He often used the simplified line—spare, with no superfluous ornamentation—that he had learned from Japanese art.

By now Vincent had completely mastered his art. He no longer looked for the right direction. He had found it. Having perfected his style, he was one of the great masters in the history of art.

Typically, Vincent chose the sunflower as the subject for many paintings—a bright yellow against various contrasting backgrounds. It almost seemed as if the painter wanted to steal a spark of fire from the sun and set it amid flower petals, to conquer once and for all a fear of darkness and of life's sorrows. But the other subjects continued as well—those portraits of café life and the famous *Starry Night on the Rhone* that Vincent finished in the company of Eugene Boch, a Belgian painter.

On September 18, Vincent finished work on the Yellow House, all repainted as he wanted. Tremendously excited, he wrote again to Gauguin, who up till now had declined Vincent's invitation to come to Arles. "Now, Paul, you won't be able to say

no. The Yellow House is finished and so you must come and come right away. I'm expecting you impatiently."

The letter found Gauguin in a receptive mood. Why should he not, like Vincent, find his artistic vocation in the South of France? He decided to find out.

In October, Gauguin arrived in Arles. The two painters resumed their discussions of the creative vision in art, and each inspired the other to do fresh work.

Vincent did two similar still lifes—his chair in the Yellow House, and Gauguin's chair. He described them in a letter to Theo as "a study of mine of a lighted candle and two novels (one yellow and the other pink) lying on an empty armchair (really Gaugin's chair), a canvas in red and green. I have been working again today at its counterpart, my own empty chair, a chair of white wood with a pipe and a tobacco pouch. In these two studies, as in others, I have tried for an effect of light by means of clear color."

Vincent felt that Gauguin was bringing out the best in him and that they could go on working together indefinitely. Vincent even had an idea that Gauguin might become a kind of director of an artists' colony at the Yellow House—an atelier du Midi, or school of the South of France—to which other artists would be invited. What if Seurat and Bernard and Toulouse-Lautrec should come!

Unfortunately, Gauguin did not feel the same way. He did not discover his artistic direction in Arles. That would not come until his visit to Tahiti, where he would find what he was seeking in the primitive life of the South Sea Islands.

Moreover, there was a clash of temperaments. Vincent was a passionate painter who worked quickly, throwing himself on a canvas and filling it in with broad strokes. Gauguin was a slow worker who stared at a canvas until his ideas came into focus, and only then would he start to paint.

Finally, Gauguin was not taken with the idea of an art colony in the Yellow House. He was too much of an individualist to work with other painters in a group.

As a result, he and Vincent began to quarrel. One time they even came to blows. However, they made up and continued together for a while longer.

Vincent continued to paint from dawn to dusk and into the night; he was turning out one masterpiece after another. But he was also smoking and drinking a lot, and the combination gave him a bad cough. He constantly brushed his eyes, which burned all the time. He had trouble sleeping.

In December, 1888, Gauguin and he decided to go to the museum in Montpellier to see the Bruyas Collection, a celebrated gathering of works by the Old Masters.

Vincent was excited by Delacroix's portraits and began to recite some verses by the poet Alfred de Musset.

Gauguin scoffed. "Delacroix is an old-fashioned academic who's been dead for years. He's the type of artist we should get away from!"

Back at the Yellow House, the spirited disagreement between the friends began to take the form of a violent row. Perhaps neither one of them meant to unleash so much anger and hostility, but the clash was between two opposing worlds: two completely different concepts of art and two rebellious and unyielding natures. Gauguin was too much of a skeptic to stand Vincent's moralism.

Things reached a melodramatic climax when Gauguin began to shout. "Fine, think as you like. But I'm fed up with Arles, with you, and with your ridiculous atelier. I'm leaving. I've made up my mind. I'm going back to Paris. Right away. Tomorrow!"

This threat caused Vincent to go into a rage. He screamed, "You can't go! I've counted too much on your being here! What's to become of the Yellow House?"

"You can still live here," Gauguin said coldly. "You can go on painting. The art colony is a myth. Nobody will come. Why should Seurat and Toulouse-Lautrec come all the way down here just because you want them to?"

"We can all work together!" Vincent yelled.

Gauguin laughed. "It would be like a lot of caterwauling cats! No thanks, it's not for me!"

Something snapped in Vincent's mind. He attacked Gauguin, who fled unharmed to a hotel.

During the night of December 22, Vincent suffered an attack of insanity, in the midst of which he cut off the lobe of one ear, wrapped it in a newspaper, and delivered it to a prostitute (who may have been another reason for the Vincent-Gauguin estrangement). The next morning he was found at home and taken to the hospital.

Vincent's mental problem has never been completely diagnosed. It may have been epilepsy or schizophrenia, as some psychiatrists now interpret the symptoms.

In any case, this tragedy produced another masterpiece. When Vincent returned to the Yellow House, he did a self-portrait complete with the bandage on his ear. This work is one of his most admired canvases.

Gauguin, naturally, would not resume his partnership with Vincent, who would have to go on painting by himself.

Mental Problems and the Last Great Paintings

For Vincent, life now became a series of seizures interspersed with periods of sanity. His seizures were so frightening to the public that, in March, 1889, a petition signed by eighty residents of Arles caused him to be returned to the hospital. Here he painted the portrait of his physician, Dr. Felix Rey, that hangs in a museum in Moscow. Here also he heard that Theo had been married in Paris.

His confinement in an asylum at nearby Saint-Rémy early in May was at his own request; he realized how far advanced his mania was. Yet he continued to paint in the asylum. Such canvases as A *Road with Cypresse and Stars* and *Cornfield with Reaper* reflect his mania in their wild, disordered brush strokes. He was seeing the world through a feverish imagination.

Two things that happened in 1890 gave Van Gogh some satisfaction. A French art critic wrote the only review of his work that appeared during his lifetime; it was an extremely complimentary review. And his picture *The Red Vineyard* became the only one, of the hundreds he painted or drew to be sold in the open market while he was alive. Vincent hoped that this sale would be the forerunner of many more. But this was not to be until after his death. Within a few decades, the sale of a single painting would have made him extremely rich, but he could know nothing of this.

All along Van Gogh had been sending pictures to Theo in Paris, but since only one had been sold, there was not enough money returning to Arles to maintain him financially. He remained dependent on Theo, as he had for so long—a fact that gave him a bad conscience to add to the rest of his psychological problems.

Vincent wrote to his brother, "Please, Theo, bring me back up north. The sun here in the Midi is blinding my eyes and driving me crazy. And I have to spend so much time in bed with a doctor leaning over me. I'm sure I'll be better in Paris."

Unfortunately, Theo, who was about to become a father, could not leave his wife just then. But the move became possible after Vincent's nephew was born (and named after him).

Vincent arrived in Paris on May 17, 1890. He enjoyed meeting his sister-in-law and nephew and talking at length with Theo. He was obstinate about one thing: he would not return to Arles. At the same time, he could not be left to himself in his condition. Theo solved the problem by renting him a hotel room in Auvers-sur-Oise, near Paris, placing him in the care of a specialist, Dr. Paul-Ferdinand Gachet.

Vincent enjoyed his new surroundings. Gachet was a student of mental problems, so he was able to help his patient through the worst crises. He also was an art lover, and he appreciated Vincent's genius. The patient, in his moments of sanity, did portraits of the doctor and the doctor's daughter along with some landscapes of Auvers and a few scenes based on his memories of life in Holland.

Occasionally Vincent was well enough to return to Paris for reunions with Theo and his family. But Paris was not the same for him as it had been in his younger days. He saw few of his old friends. Most of the Impressionists were scattered in pursuit of their own vocations, and many were not even aware that he was in Paris.

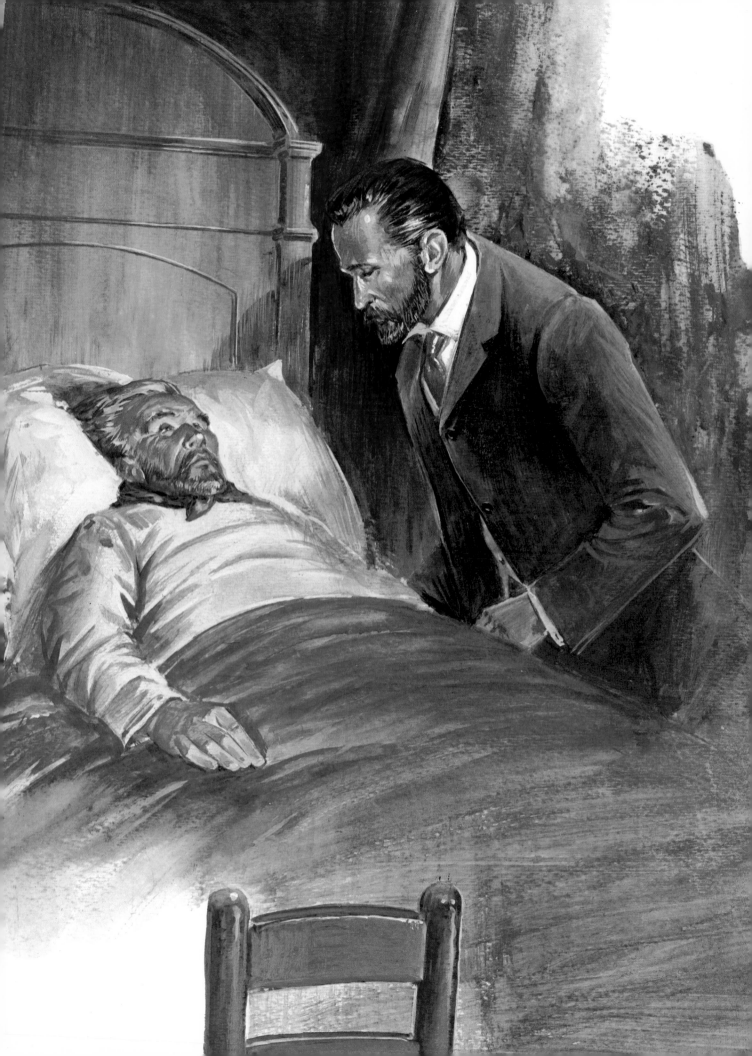

He was lonelier than ever. He made acquaintances in Paris, but no real friends, and Theo, with his family duties, could not give him as much attention as in the past.

While Vincent continued to paint during his good spells, his bad spells were becoming more frequent. He became obsessed with the thought that he was a financial burden on Theo, even though Theo assured him that there was sufficient money to take care of all Vincent's expenses without making Theo's family suffer.

Working on his last paintings, Vincent said that he "tried to express extreme solitude and melancholy." Such were his feelings in the final days of his life.

On July 27, 1890, he shot himself in the abdomen with a revolver. He was found unconscious in his room, but he regained consciousness and was even able to sit up in bed. Dr. Gachet even thought he might survive.

The news of the shooting brought Theo hurrying out to Auvers from Paris. The two brothers had an emotional reunion. They talked about their future, if Vincent recovered.

Vincent did not recover, however. He died on July 29, 1890. Theo, together with a few friends, made up the funeral procession accompanying the body to the Auvers Cemetery. The painters Émile Bernard and Camille Pissarro were among the mourners.

Theo died six months later. Eventually, he was buried beside his brother in the Auvers Cemetery. Fittingly, they still lie there together, as close in death as they were in life.

Time has done justice to Vincent van Gogh. If his strange, agitated way of painting struck his contemporaries as crude and violent, unsuitable for livingroom walls, critics and art lovers since then have come to understand and appreciate his genius and ability to give all of nature—the good and bad, the idyllic or painful, the day and the night—a human dimension. Vincent's voice is still with us as much in his letters as in his artwork. He wrote: "The [cypress] tree is as beautiful of line and proportion as an Egyptian obelisk." And, "What happiness....I've stayed up three nights in a row to paint. Sometimes I think that the night is much more alive and colorful than the day." And when he was unhappy he would confess, "The wheat fields extend on forever under a stormy sky, and I have no trouble recreating the sadness and extreme loneliness."

Today humanity understands what he meant, what he was trying to do and the marvelous extent to which he succeeded in expressing his artistic vision. That is why there is no more popular artist than Vincent van Gogh.

BUT WHO WERE THE IMPRESSIONISTS? HOW DID THEY GET THEIR NAME?

On April 25, 1874, a group of artists held their first collective exhibition in the studio of a photographer named Nadar at 35 Boulevard des Capucines in Paris. Their official name was The Anonymous Society of Artists, Painters, Sculptors, and Engravers, and the members included many now-famous painters—Monet, Pissarro, Degas, Cézanne, Sisley, and Renoir. At that first show, the public reacted very negatively to their work. One painting by Claude Monet, entitled *Impression: Rising Sun* (1872), spurred an amused critic to coin the word *Impressionism* to describe the artists' new way of painting and, specifically, their ability to capture a "fleeting" visual sensation. Art for these painters was no mere imitation of reality. What mattered to them instead was the artist's perception of what was taking place before his eyes. The idea was to render this personal vision—this *impression*—on canvas. Being out in the middle of Nature went hand in hand with a sense of joy at being alive and feeling enraptured with the fragrant air and splendid light. How one looked at things depended on the light and its infinite variations; this explains why the Impressionists took to studying carefully how light changes, however slight the alteration. It was only natural that these new perceptions led to a new painting style. The artists' palettes brightened up as they eliminated all grays, blacks, and browns in favor of the purest and most brilliant hues. Their brushstrokes became more minute and flitting as they allowed the light to dissolve all contours. Figures, objects, and landscape blended—one into the next—and every aspect of reality was broken down, becoming part of the general vibrant atmosphere.

Claude Monet, *Impression: The Rising Sun*, 1872. Marmottan Museum, Paris.

THE JAPANESE INFLUENCE

Japanese art had an effect not only on Van Gogh but on most painters of that period. Their "discovery" of Japanese prints in particular signaled a change in the use of color. Instead of not trying to imitate the exotic art of the Orient, these artists merely wanted to incorporate it—along with other sources—into their search for a new approach to painting. For Vincent van Gogh, moreover, the Eastern art he came upon served to confirm his personal observations on nature. He wrote the following opinions at various times:

All my work is based on Japanese prints.

The art of Japan, while on the decline in that country, has put down roots in the work of the French Impressionists.

Is it not a sort of religion, that which the Japanese are trying to teach us, living in Nature as if they too were simple flowers? I don't think it's possible to study Japanese art without feeling happier and more cheerful. It forces us to return to Nature despite all our upbringing and work determined by a conventionalized world.

Vincent van Gogh, *Japanese Period: Bridge Under the Rain*, 1887. National Museum V. van Gogh, Amsterdam.

Ando Hiroshige
Ohashi Under the Rain
(part of the wood-carving series A *Hundred Views of Edo*, 1856–1858).
Guimet Museum, Paris.

"THE AIR IN FRANCE...DOES ME...A WORLD OF GOOD..."

"...*the air in France clarifies my thoughts and does me good, a world of good, the most good possible.*" This was one of the first thoughts Van Gogh had upon his arrival in Paris from Belgium. He was referring not only to the artistic circles he found there but also to the landscape, hues, and lighting that would have a clear influence on the use of color in his painting. The south of France, known as Provence, would become his adopted homeland. Here at last he would find—and make use of—an ideal setting for expressing the joy so infrequent in his actual life. He would discover Arles, "*the town of oleanders and sulphur sun.*" Whenever possible, Van Gogh painted outdoors in the sunlight, using nature as his model. He put aside his sketch pad the minute the wheat in a field was plowed under or the flowers started to fade. In his letters, Van Gogh wrote often of his fascination with color: "*The town seems as beautiful as Japan to me, what with its crystal-clear air and the joyous splashes of color. The water creates spots of beautiful emerald green and rich blue just like in the landscapes I've seen painted on cloth. The orange sunsets make the ground look blue. The sun is a brilliant yellow.*"

Vincent van Gogh, *The Bridge at Langlois*, 1888.
Wallraf-Richartz Museum, Cologne.

Vincent van Gogh,
Fishing Boats on the Beach at Saintes-Maries, 1888.
National Museum V. van Gogh, Amsterdam.

VINCENT VAN GOGH AND FRENCH IMPRESSIONISM

Even if Vincent van Gogh is usually included together with the Impressionists, a closer look reveals just how independent and unique an artist he actually was.

Evidence of his originality—which defies all easy classification—can be found in the letters he wrote to his brother Theo. For instance, these paragraphs are from a letter mailed from Arles in August, 1888.

I'm finding that what I learned in Paris is leaving me, and that I'm returning instead to those ideas I had out in the countryside before ever meeting the Impressionists. I wouldn't be surprised if they started making comments about my technique, which has been influenced less by them and more by Delacroix.

What I'm trying to do, in fact, is not to faithfully imitate on canvas what I see before me but rather to use color in the most arbitrary way in order to express myself better. But enough of this theoretical talk: let me give you an example of what I mean.

I want to paint the portrait of an artist friend who dreams big dreams and paints the way a nightingale sings just because he's like that by Nature. He is blond. And I want to put into the painting all the admiration and affection I feel for him. I'll paint him exactly as he is, as close to real life as I can—at first. But the picture is far from finished at this point. To finish it, I must now make radical use of color. I will exaggerate his blondness; the hair will take on orange hues, or cream, or a soft lemon yellow. Behind his head, I don't want to show the drab wall of his miserable apartment but rather the firmament, a background of nothing but the most intense and violent cobalt blue I can come up with. And this combination of his blond head illuminated against a dark cobalt background will have a mysterious effect: it will resemble a star in the deep blue sky.

(from *Van Gogh*: Vol. II, Rizzoli, Milan, Italy)

Vincent van Gogh,
Portrait of Dr. Gachet, 1890.
The Louvre, Paris.

Crimean War, the battle on the Cernaia River in which the soldiers from Piedmont (Italy) fought so valiantly.

CHRONOLOGY	
Life of Vincent van Gogh	**Historical and Cultural Events**
1853 March 30 — A son is born to the Reverend Theodorus van Gogh and his wife Anna Cornelia Carbentus in Groot Zundert in the Brabant region of Holland. He is called Vincent Willem, after the still-born baby born to Anna Cornelia the previous year.	**1853** Events in Russia and Turkey set the stage for the outbreak of the Crimean War (1854-1856).
1857 May 1 — Theodorus "Theo" van Gogh is born. Vincent will be very close to his brother until the end of his tormented life.	
	1858 Lincoln-Douglas debates held in Illinois.
1859 Vincent, an unruly and solitary child, completes his first drawings, which his mother treasures.	**1859** Construction begins on the Suez Canal, according to plans drawn up by Ferdinand de Lesseps.
	1861 In America, the Civil War between the North and the South begins over the issue of slavery.
	1863 Lincoln issues the Emancipation Proclamation. Battle of Gettysburg fought.
1864 October 1 — Vincent enters the school headed by Jean Provily in Zevenbergen. There he studies French, English, and German.	**1864** The International Red Cross is founded in Switzerland through the efforts of Henri Dunant.
	1865 April 9 — Robert E. Lee surrenders at Appomattox. April 14 — President Lincoln shot.
	1867 In Mexico, the Republican forces occupy Queretaro, and upon orders from B.

Suez Canal. Construction began in 1859, and the canal was opened in 1869.

The composer Richard Wagner in a photograph by Bonnet.

The Battle of Gettysburg during the American Civil War.

Life of Vincent van Gogh	Historical and Cultural Events
	Juarez, they execute Maximilian of Austria, the emperor of Mexico.
1868 Due to the family's financial problems and also to his poor grades, Vincent leaves school and returns to Groot Zundert.	**1868** President Andrew Johnson impeached and acquitted. Opening of Suez Canal. Completion of Transcontinental Railroad.
1869 July 30 — He leaves for The Hague to begin his apprenticeship with the art gallery of Goupil & Cie.	**1869** Publication of *L'Education Sentimentale* by French author Gustave Flaubert.
	1870 The novelist Charles Dickens dies in London. He is remembered for the realism and humor found in his works. Napoleon III declares war on Prussia and the Franco-Prussian War begins.
1871 Vincent spends his vacation in Helvoirt, where his family is now living.	**1871** Chicago fire destroys most of the city.
1873 January — Theo van Gogh is hired by Goupil & Cie. in their Brussels branch. May — Vincent is transferred to Goupil's London branch. His acquaintance with a young woman ends sadly. After a brief stay at home with his family, he returns to London with his sister Anna.	
1874 Vincent is transferred to Goupil's main office in Paris.	**1874** Art exhibition held in Paris by a group of artists known as the Impressionists. Heinrich Schliemann begins archaeological excavations on the site of the ancient city of Mycenae, Greece.

Illustrations from the title page of *The Pickwick Papers*, a novel by Charles Dickens.

Napoleon III and Empress Eugénie descending the grand staircase at the Tuileries.

Paris, 1871: Soldiers who were sent to put down the revolt join the rebel forces.

"The Lion Gate," principal entrance into Mycenae, was excavated by Schliemann.

Life of Vincent van Gogh	Historical and Cultural Events
	1875 Albert Schweitzer is born in Alsace. He will become a noted physician-missionary in Africa.
1876 Vincent is dismissed from his job and moves to Ramsgate, England, where he works as a teacher. November — Becomes an assistant to the preacher in a Methodist church in a working-class area on the outskirts of London.	**1876** Bell and Bray start manufacturing telephones on an industrial scale in America. Massacre of Custer's troops by Sitting Bull at the Battle of the Little Big Horn.
1877 Goes to Amsterdam to study theology.	**1877** Thomas Edison invents the phonograph.
1878 Vincent attends the Flemish Evangelical School in Brussels, where he is judged unfit for the ministry. He moves to Borinage, a mining area in southern Belgium, and tries to help the miners.	
1879 Vincent is given a probationary appointment (which is not renewed) as a lay preacher among the miners.	**1879** Thomas Edison produces the first electric light bulb. Siemens constructs the first railroad to use electric trains.
1880 Realizes his vocation as an artist and settles in Brussels. Enters the Academy of Fine Arts there.	**1880** The death of the French writer Gustave Flaubert, one of the greatest novelists of the nineteenth century.
1881 Vincent travels to Etten, where his family now lives. He is once again spurned by a woman he loves, and decides to move to The Hague and study with the painter Anton Mauve.	**1881** Pablo Picasso is born in Malaga, Spain. He will be considered one of the greatest twentieth century painters. Construction of Panama Canal begins.
1882 June — Hospitalized with an infectious disease.	**1882** The Triple Alliance is formed between Germany, Austria-Hungary, and Italy.

One of the first telephones, soon to be common throughout the world.

Thomas Edison sitting next to his phonograph.

The French novelist Gustave Flaubert in a painting by E. Giraud.

A medallion of the Triple Alliance, showing the three heads of state: William I, Humbert I, and Francis Joseph I.

Life of Vincent van Gogh	Historical and Cultural Events
1883 Following a turbulent period, he winds up at his parents' home, now located in Nuenen, Belgium, and paints continuously.	**1883** Brooklyn Bridge opens. Northern Pacific railroad completed.
1885 After his father dies, Vincent leaves Nuenen, where he has worked for two years. He moves to Antwerp. There he renews his contacts with members of the artistic circles.	**1885** Benz and Daimler manufacture a prototype car with a piston engine. Louis Pasteur administers first inoculation to protect against rabies.
1886 Following a serious illness, he leaves Antwerp and goes to live with Theo in Paris. He meets many famous Impressionist painters and becomes friendly with Paul Gauguin.	**1886** The city of Johannesburg, South Africa is founded. Death of pianist and composer Franz Liszt. Statue of Liberty unveiled in New York Harbor.
1888 Vincent settles in Arles, in the south of France. September — He moves into the "Yellow House." October — Gauguin finally accepts Vincent's invitation to join him in Arles, but the two friends have problems living together. After a heated argument in which Vincent makes violent threats, Gauguin flees and Vincent cuts off his own ear.	**1888** During the reign of King Pedro, slavery is abolished in Brazil. This measure will incite plantation owners to overthrow the government the following year.
1889 Vincent is hospitalized several times in Arles. May — He voluntarily enters an asylum in Saint-Remy. He continues to paint.	**1889** The Eiffel Tower is completed for the Paris Exposition. Oklahoma opened for settlement.
1890 May — Vincent insists on returning to Paris. He lives in Auvers-sur-Oise, where he is treated by Dr. Gachet. July 27 — Vincent shoots himself. With Theo at his bedside, he dies two days later. He is thirty-seven years old.	**1890** In America, Dunlop makes the first inflatable rubber tires. After the German emperor William II ascends to the throne, Prince Otto von Bismarck is forced to resign as chancellor.

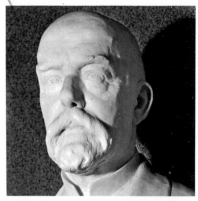

A bust of the scientist Robert Koch. Robert Koch Institute, Berlin.

One of the first Benz automobiles with three wheels.

Caricature of the pianist and composer Franz Liszt. Library of the Opèra, Paris.

The Eiffel Tower, completed in Paris in 1889.

Index

Books for Further Reading

Lust for Life, a novel by Irving Stone (1984)

Dear Theo: The Autobiography of Vincent van Gogh, a selection from the
letters of the two brothers by Irving Stone (1969)

Vincent van Gogh and His Art by Rosemary Treble (1981)

Van Gogh by Meyer Schapiro (1950)

Vincent van Gogh, 1853-1890 by Walter Pach (1936)

The Symbolic Language of Vincent van Gogh by H.R. Graetz (1963)